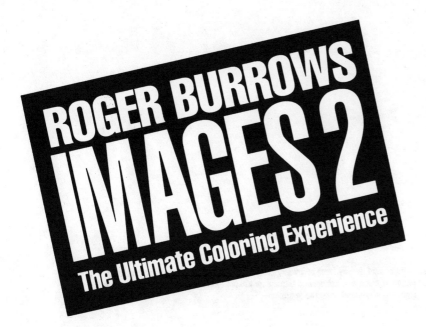

ROGER BURROWS
IMAGES 2
The Ultimate Coloring Experience

RUNNING PRESS
PHILADELPHIA · LONDON

30 29 28 27 26 25 24 23 22
Digit on the right indicates the number of this printing.

ISBN 1–56138–110–1

Cover design by Toby Schmidt
Interior design by Christian Benton
Typography: Helvetica Compressed by Commcor Communications, Philadelphia, Pennsylvania
Front and back cover artwork by Barney Schmidt
Back cover artwork by Lili Schwartz and Jon Pochos

This book may be ordered by mail from the publisher.
Please add $2.50 for postage and handling.
But try your bookstore first!
Running Press Book Publishers
125 South Twenty-second Street
Philadelphia, Pennsylvania 19103–4399

INTRODUCTION

Color provides the key to developing your imagination through <u>Images</u> designs. Colored pencils and felt-tip pens are easy to use. Watercolors and acrylics require more skill and time, but are certainly worth consideration.

Many people have rendered the designs in other media, such as tapestry, embroidery, silkscreen, and even in ceramic and vacuum-formed tiles. The largest applications have been in architectural design.

The creative potential of the <u>Images</u> designs can be unlocked by anyone. When I first developed the designs, I gave them to children to color. The resulting pictures and designs were nothing short of amazing. It was as though the lines, rather than restricting the children's imaginations, stimulated them. Even two-year-olds produced forms which they were not "supposed" to be producing until much later.

Adults, too, became inspired. People who considered themselves to have no artistic ability were suddenly producing pictures, patterns, and forms that were surprisingly good. The designs turned out to be great confidence builders.

This second collection of <u>Images</u> designs has been selected to encourage the development of imagination and creativity through the use of centered motifs. Where the full-page designs of the first book help you to see and create pictures and forms, the designs of <u>Images 2</u> encourage focusing on symmetrical shapes and patterns. The results, I believe, will be equally rewarding.

Roger Burrows is the author of twenty books and papers on geometry, design, and architectural form, and more than fifty books for children. In the early '70s he worked with Dr. Ensor Holiday, of Guys Hospital, London, to develop Altair Designs, which were variations of a particular geometrical pattern from a collection of architectural designs assembled during Napoleon's occupation of Egypt.

Mr. Burrows is currently a publishing executive with John B. Fairfax International and is based in New York. Prior to that he developed Questron, an interactive book and electronic "wand" system for children. He has also designed a number of major exhibitions in the United Kingdom, including an exhibition of futuristic designs for the investiture of the Prince of Wales, and geometrical structures for the Architectural Association in London.

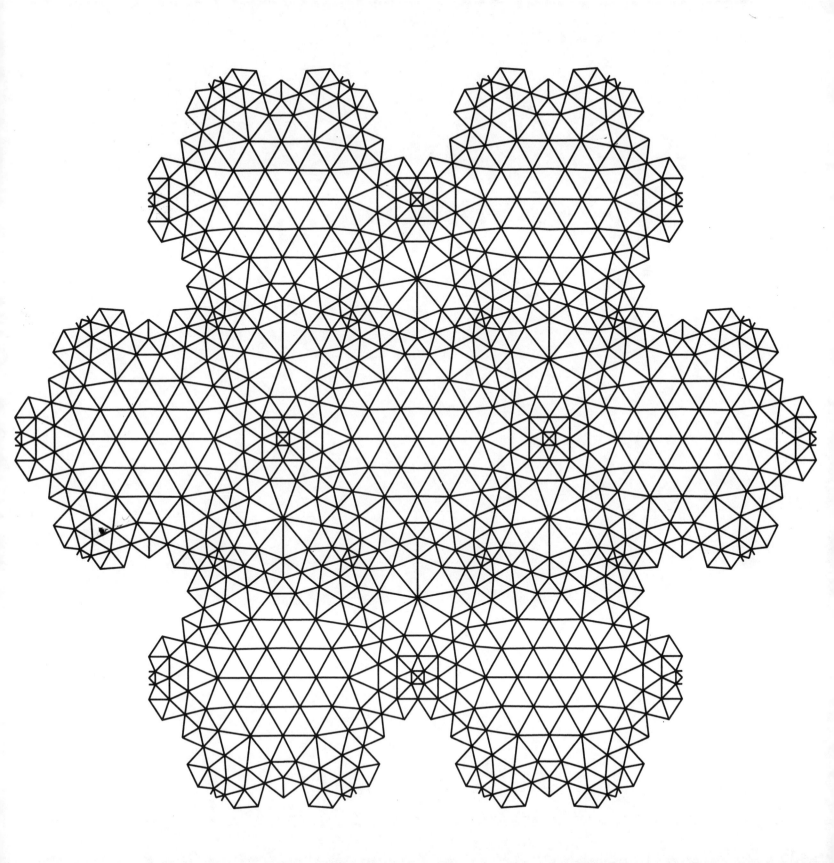

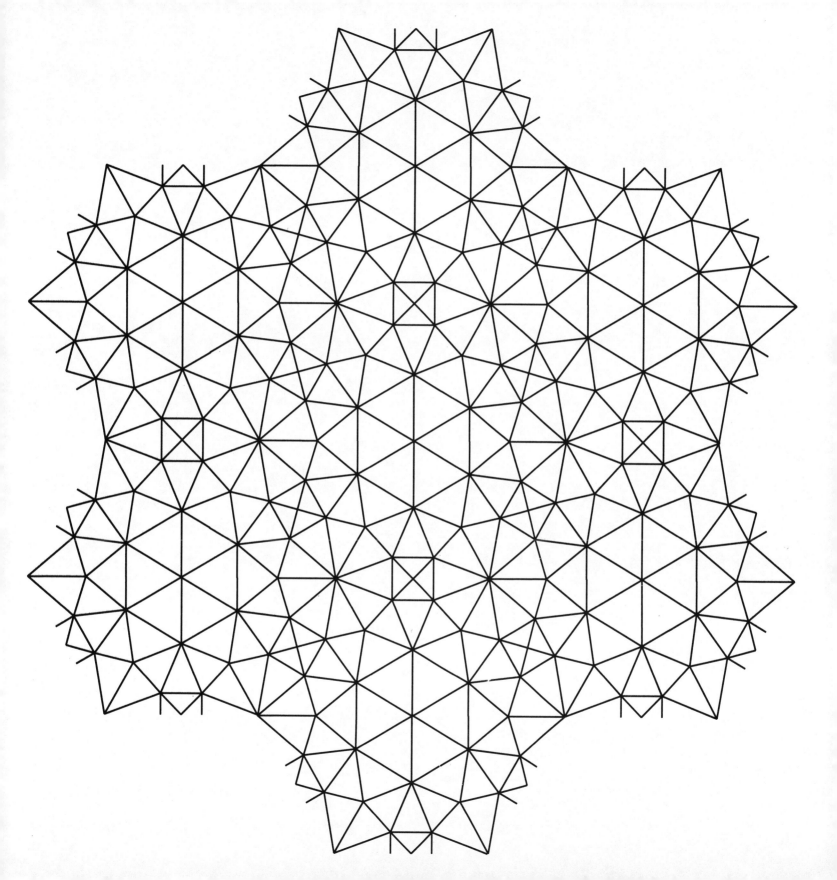

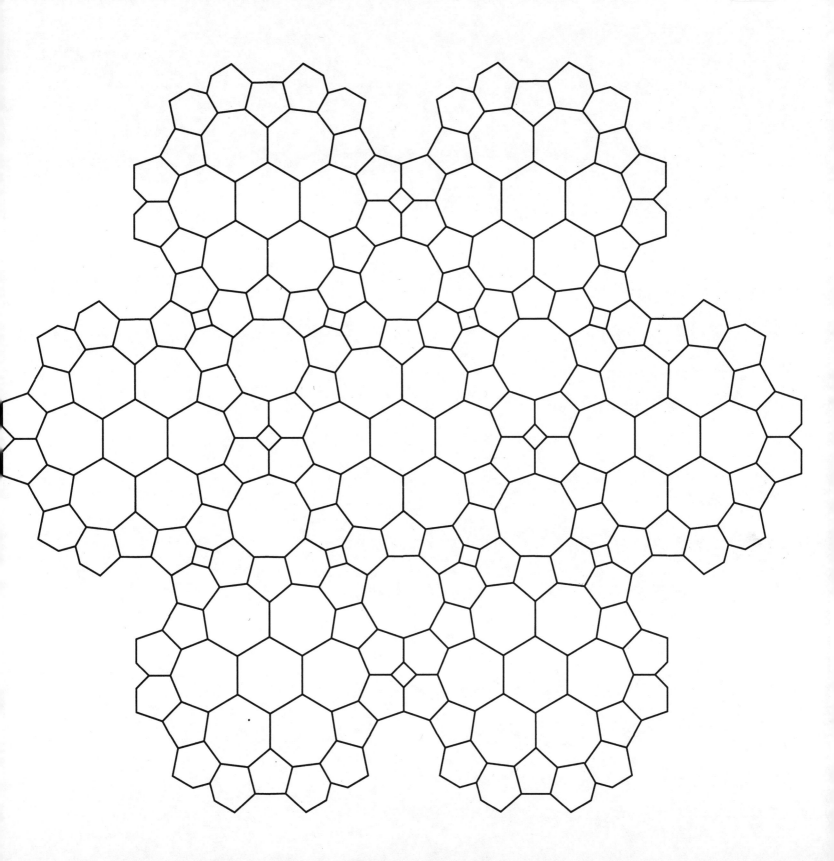

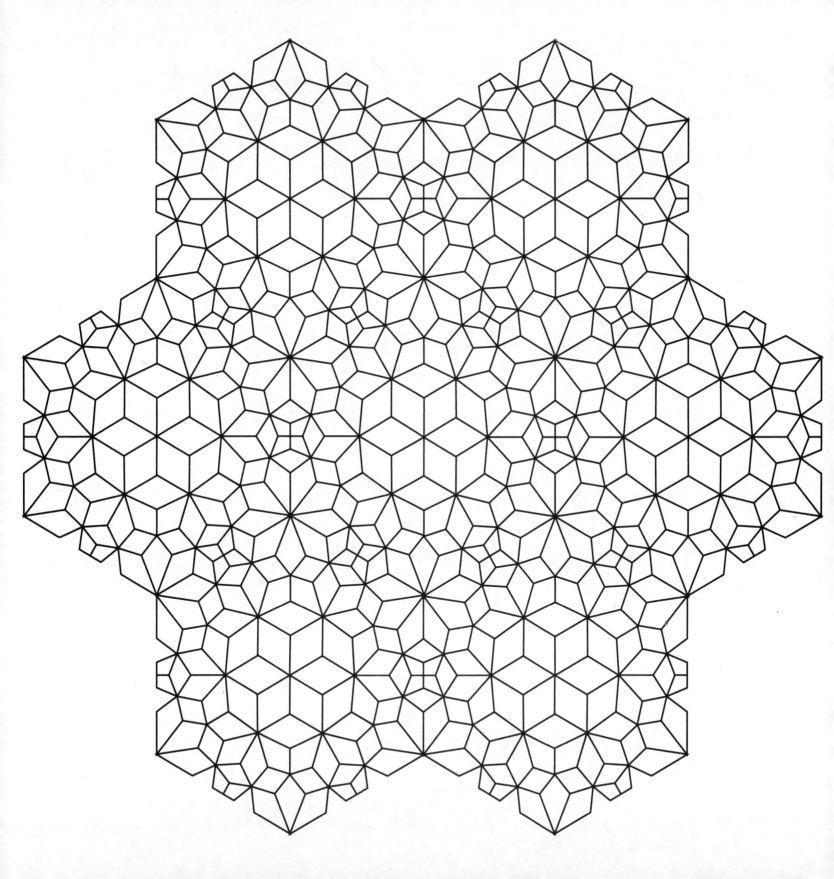

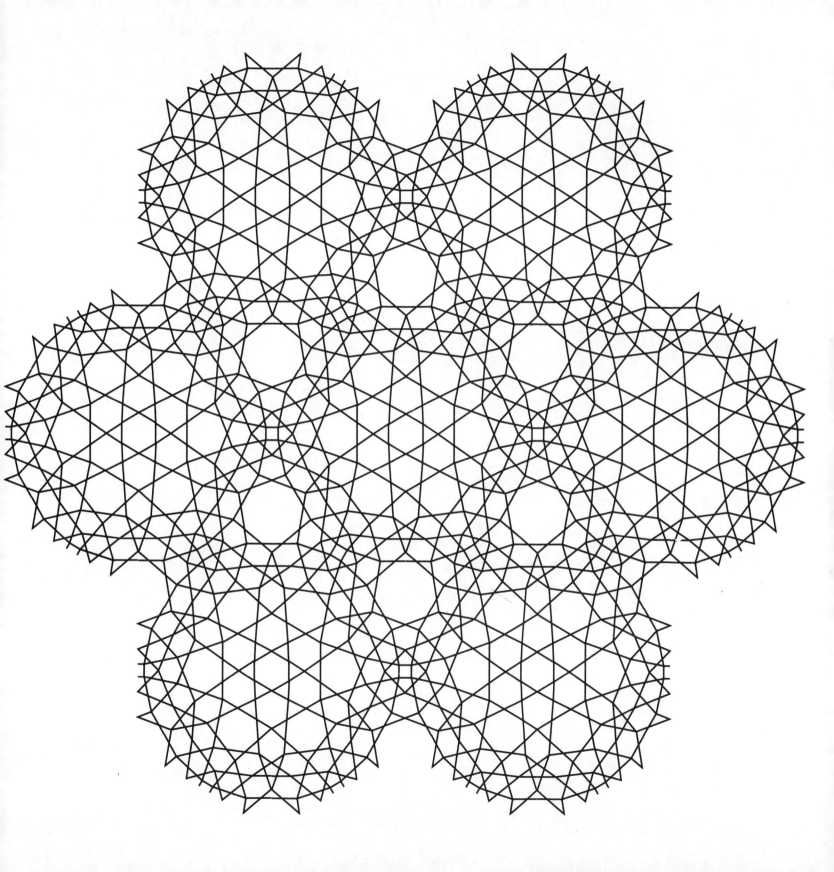

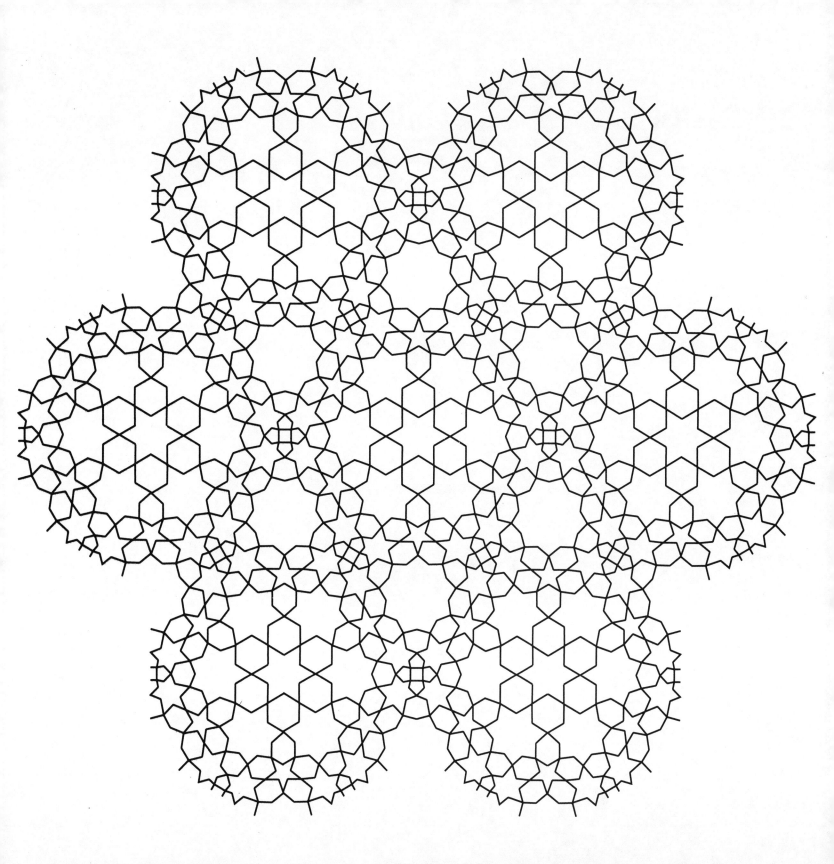

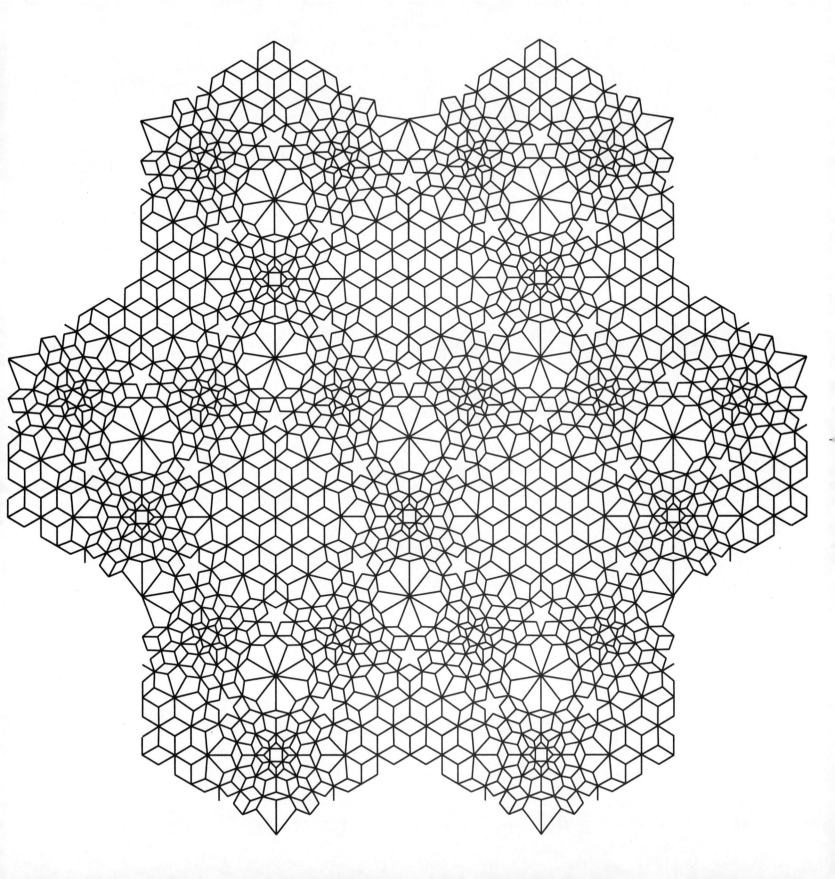

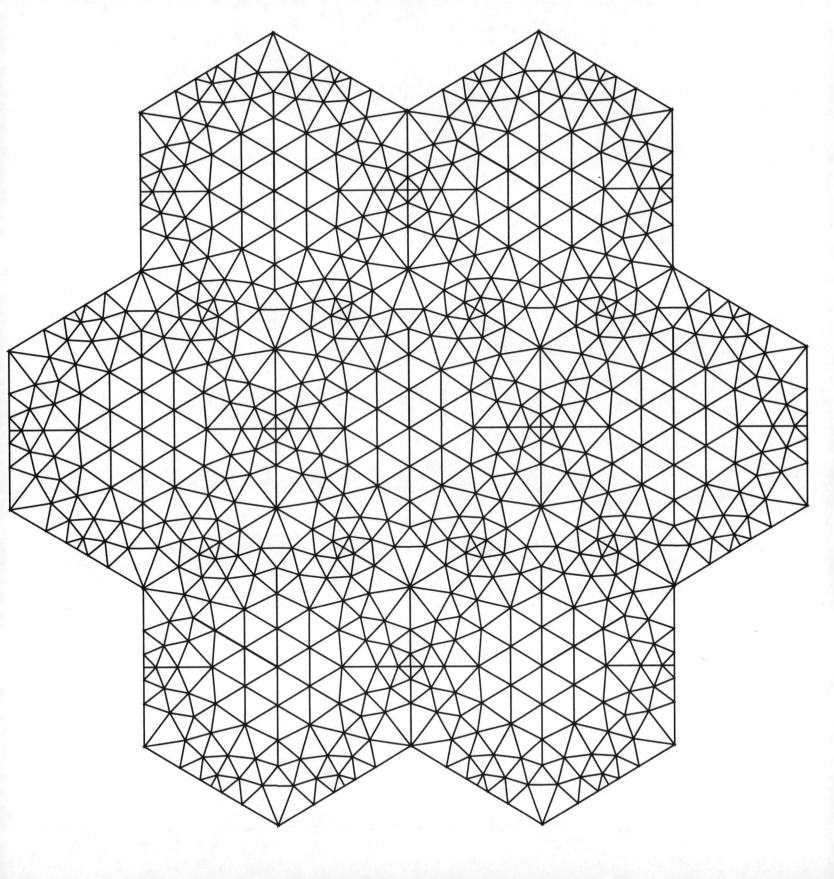

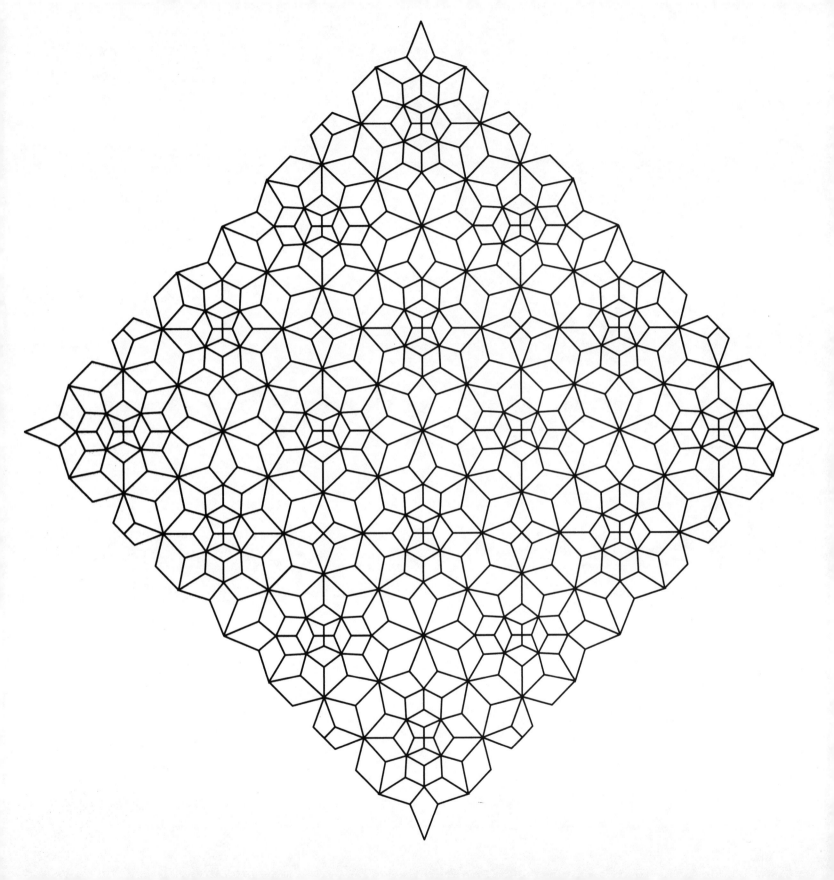

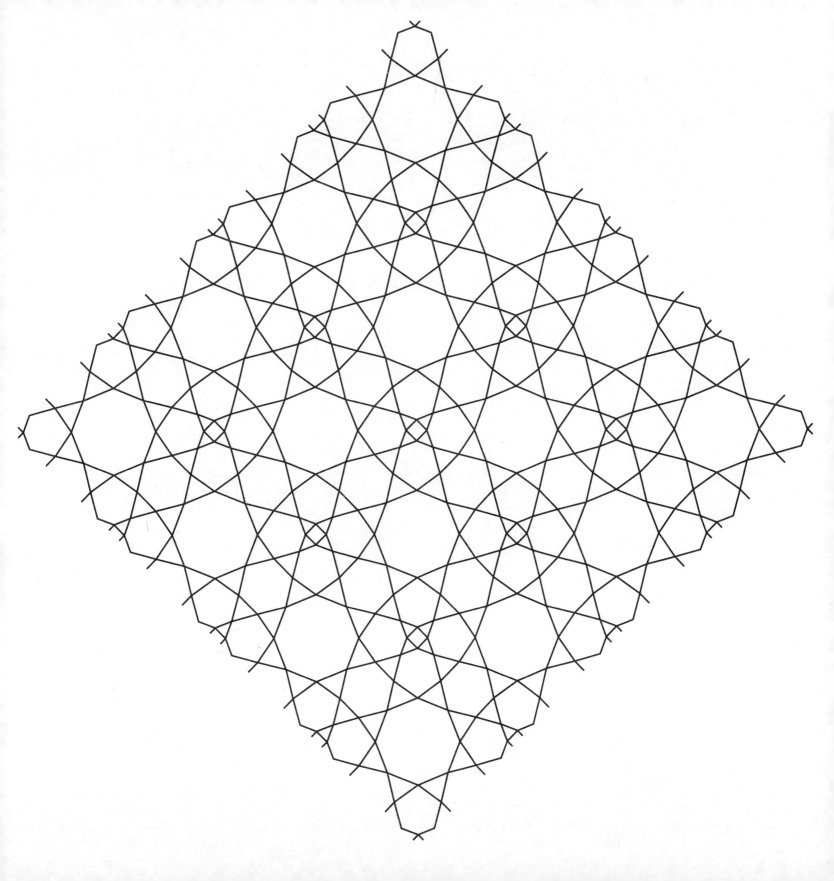

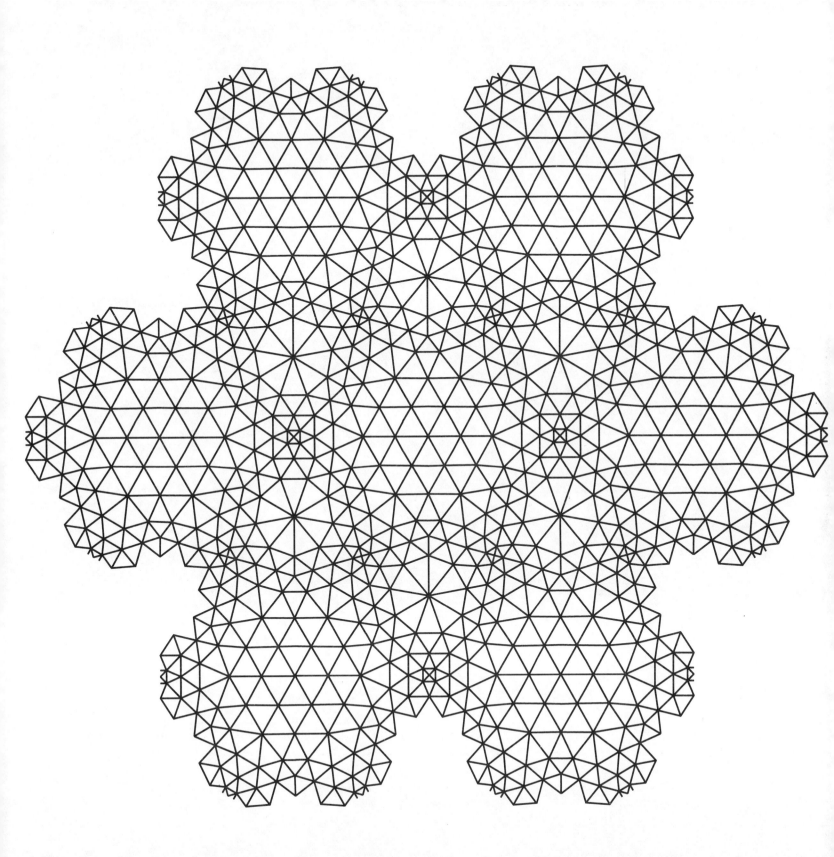

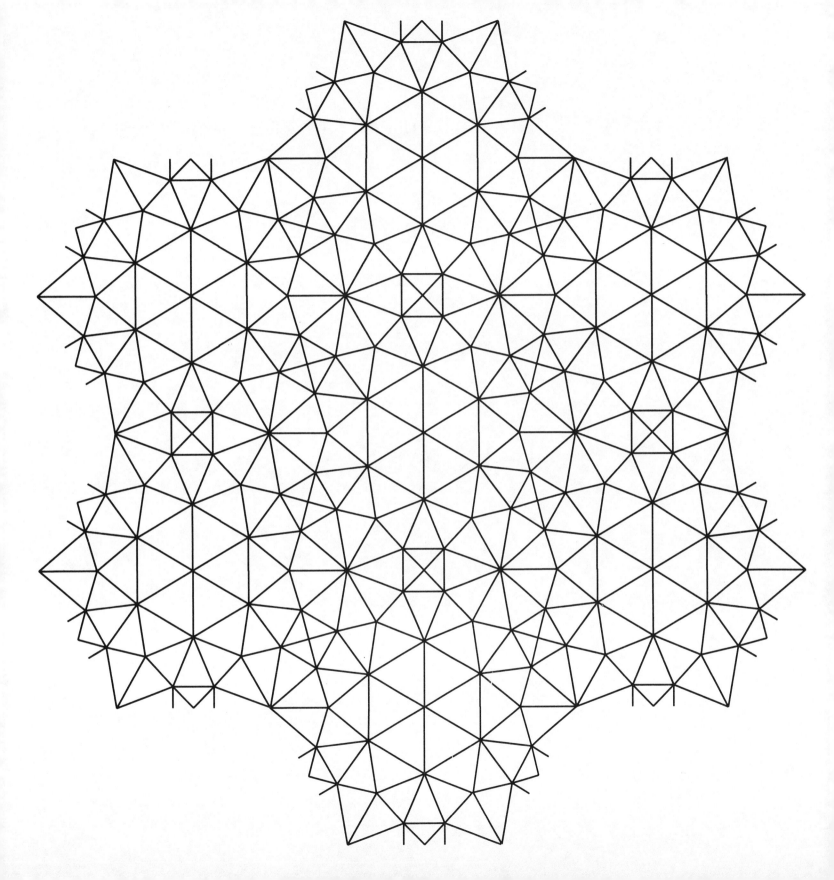

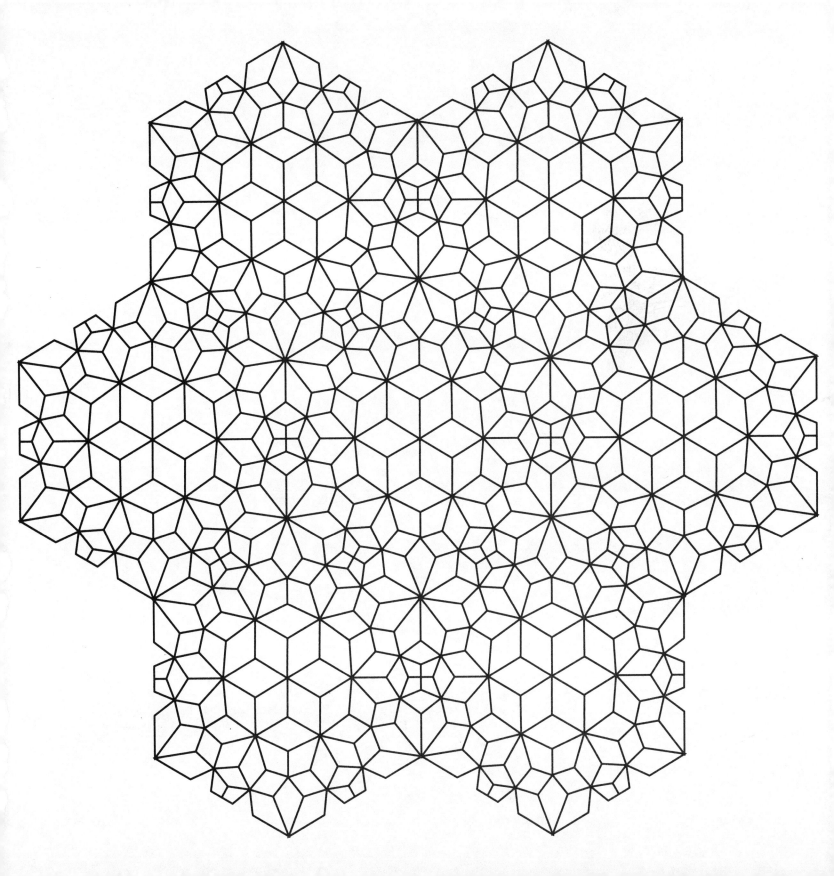

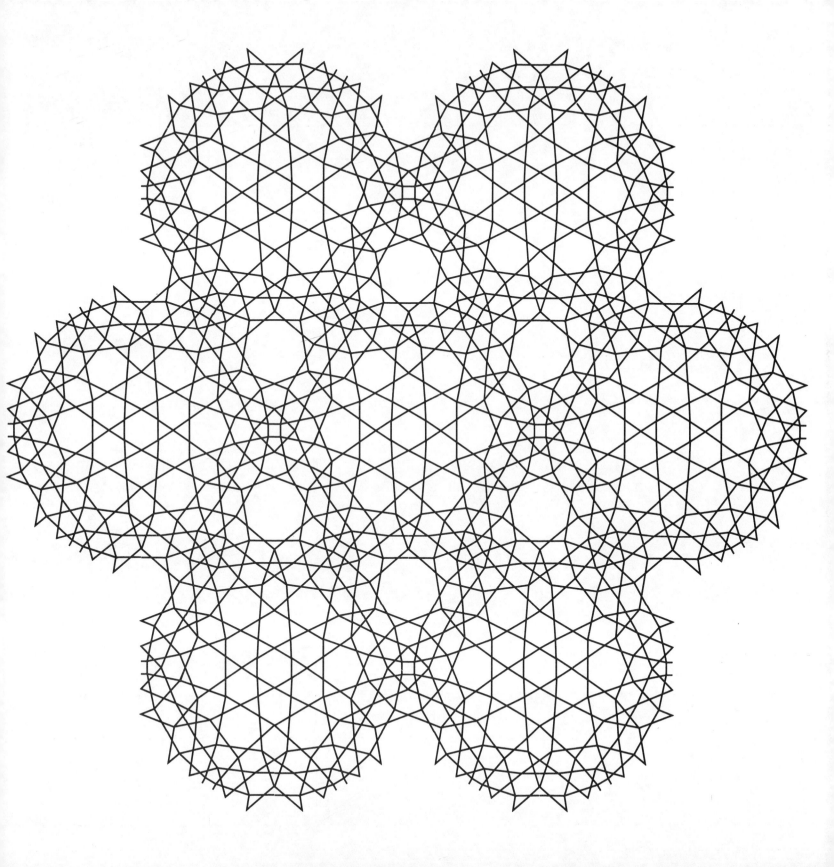

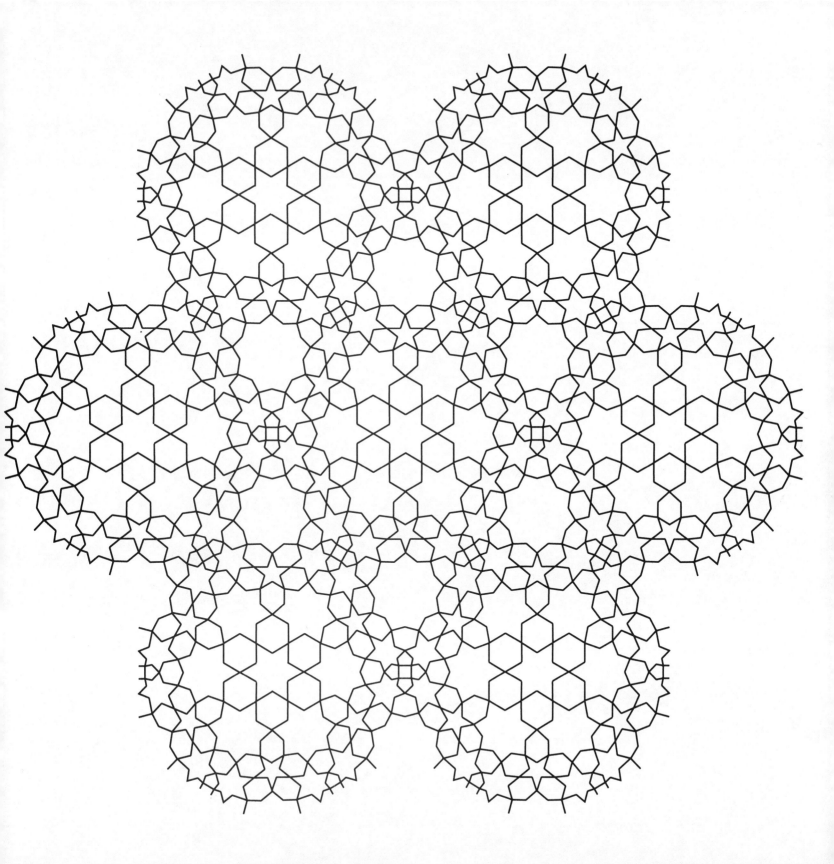

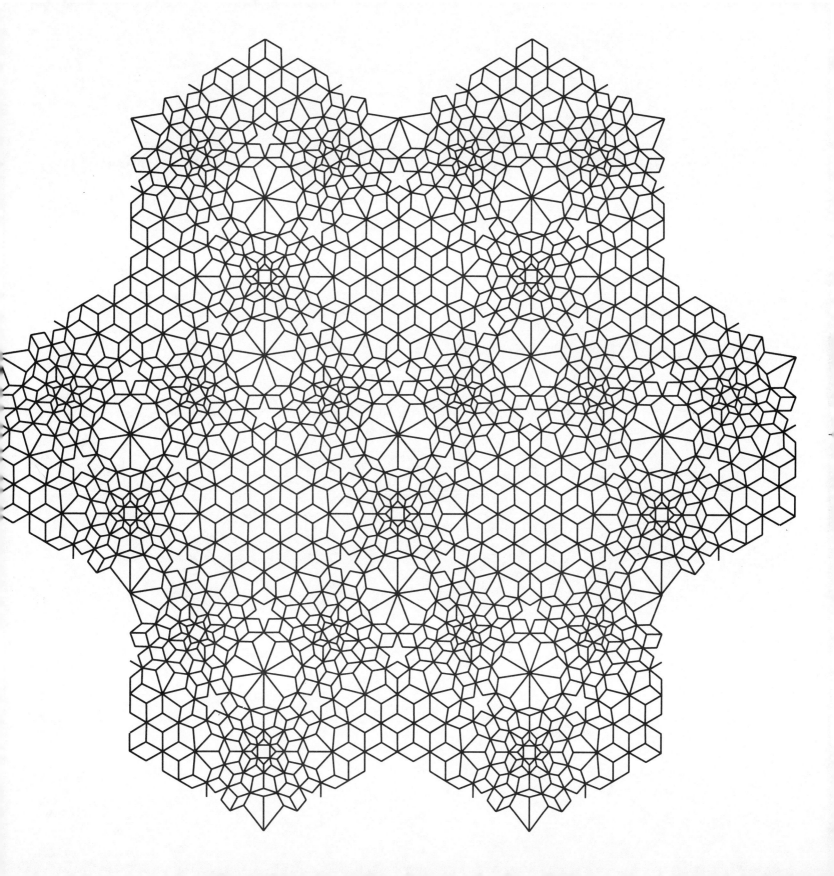

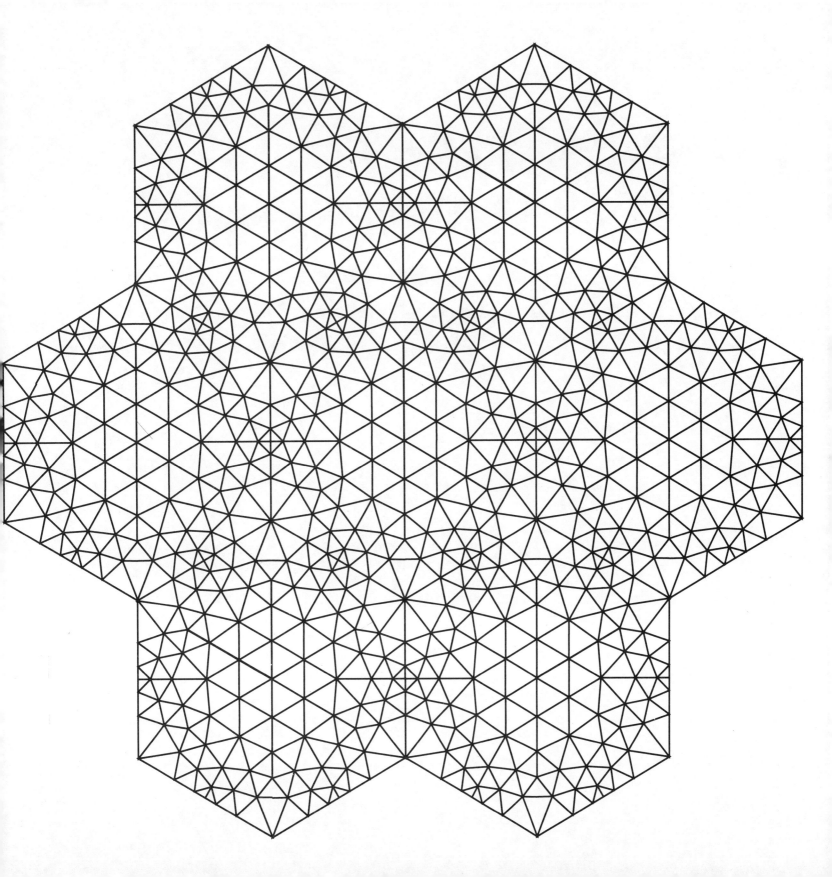

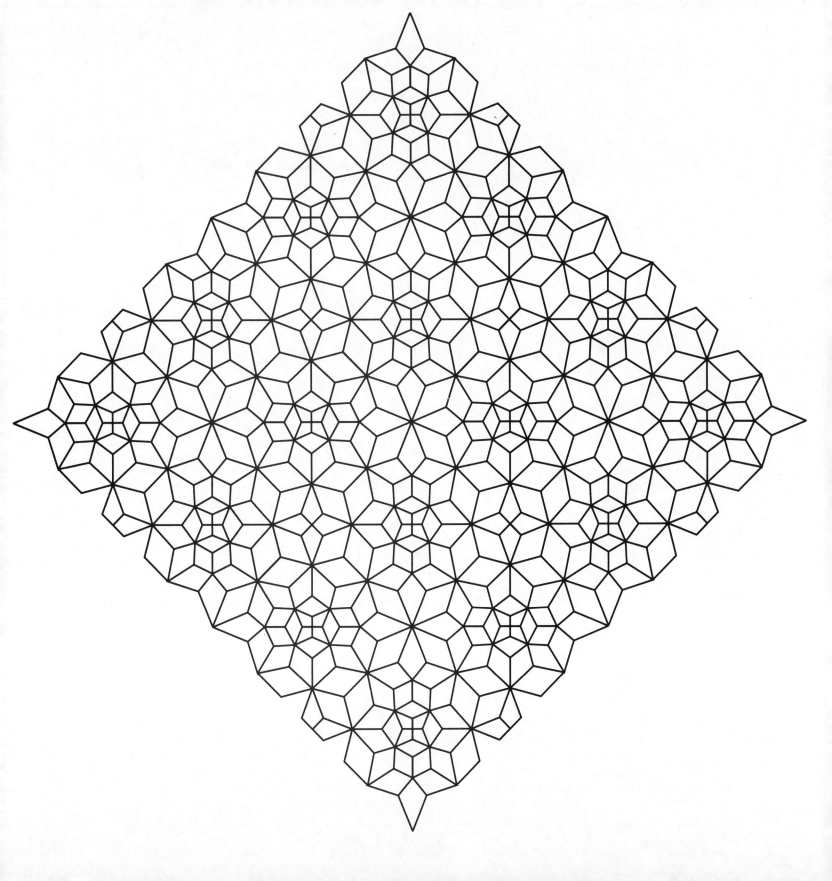

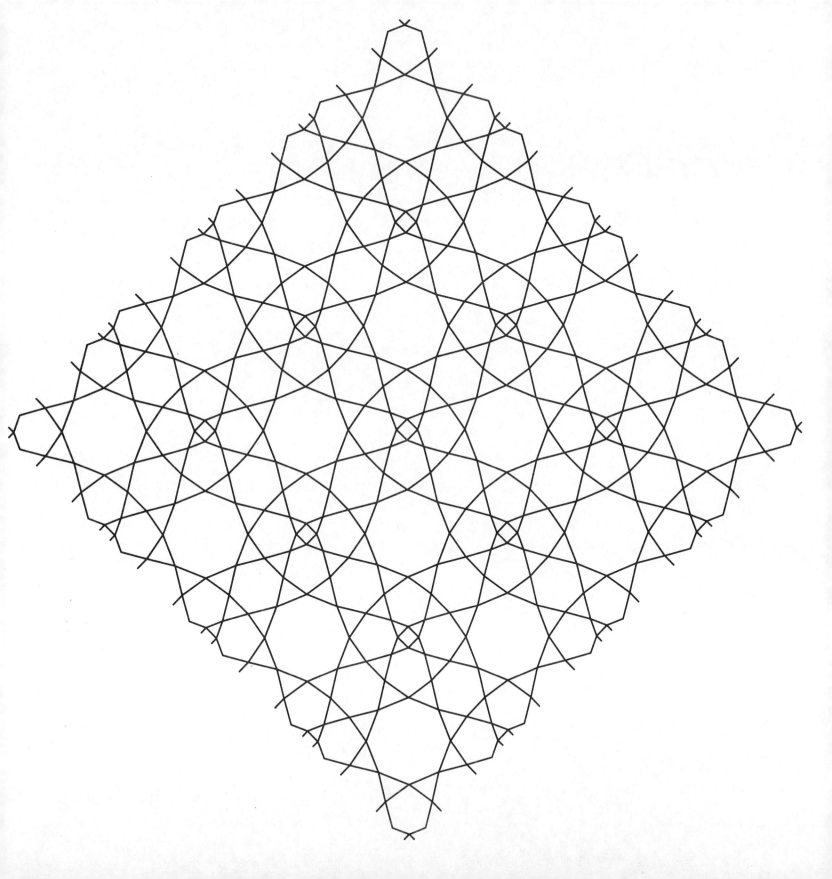

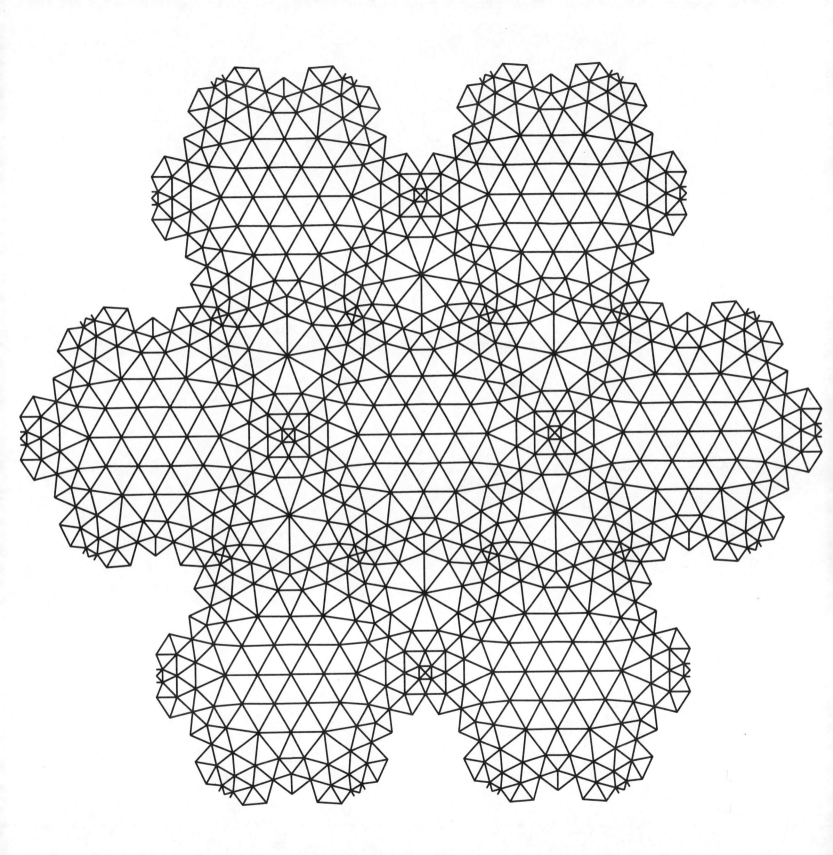

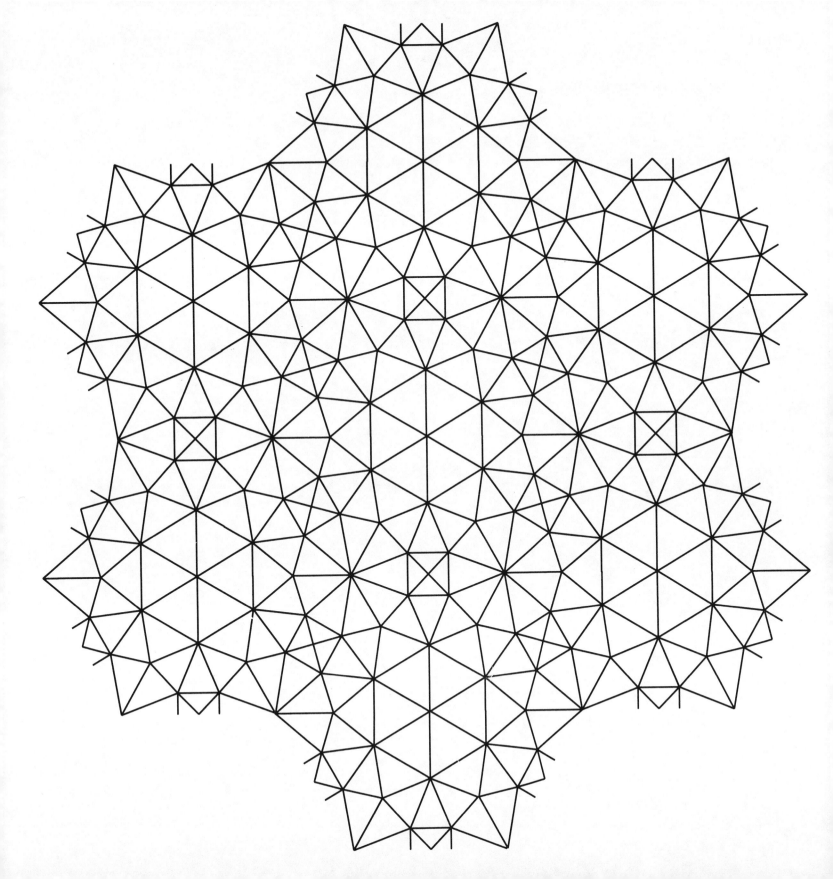

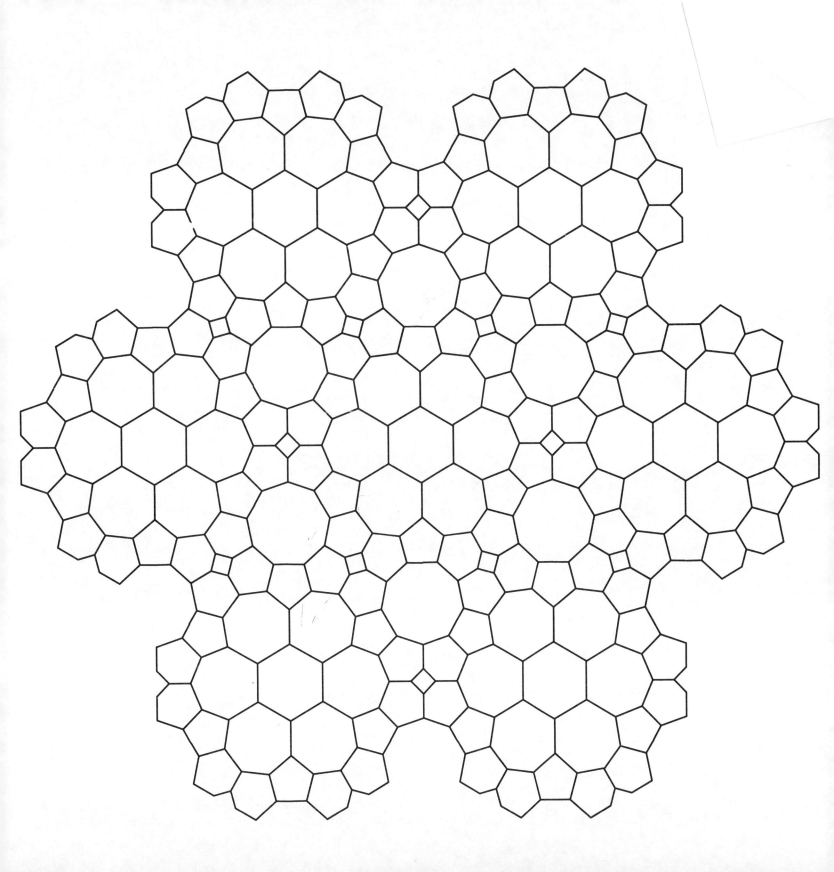

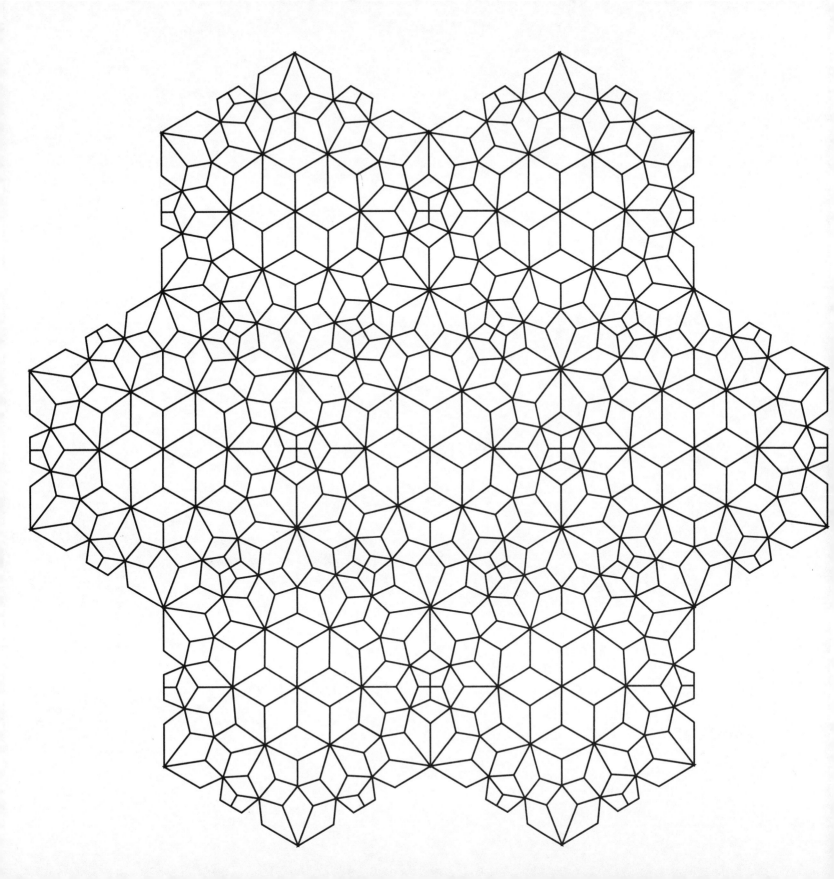

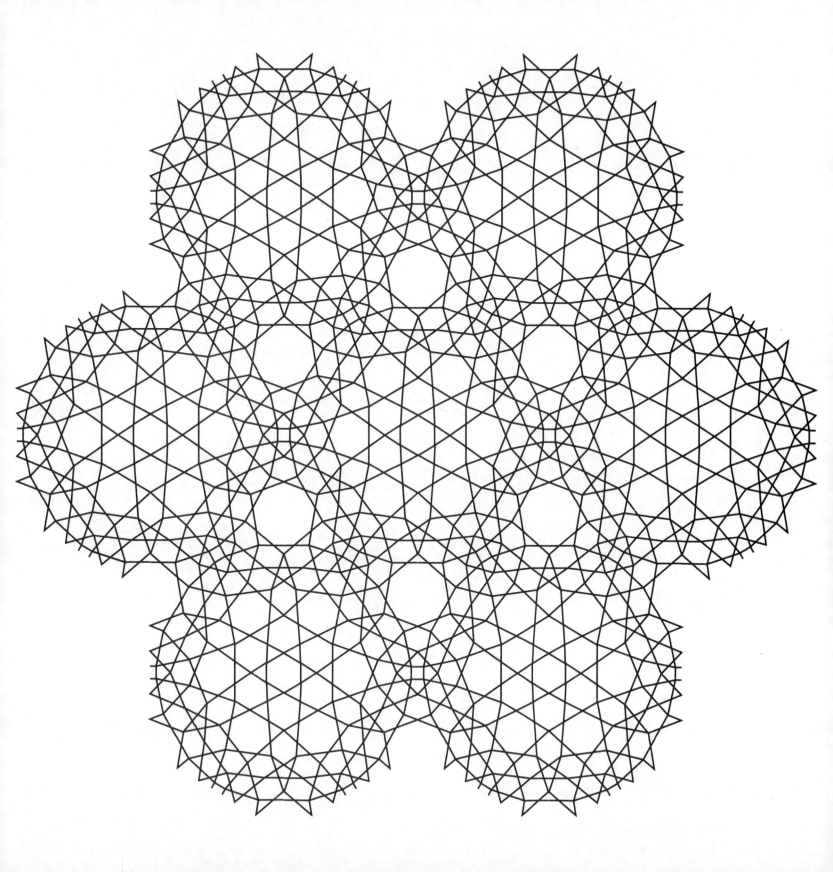

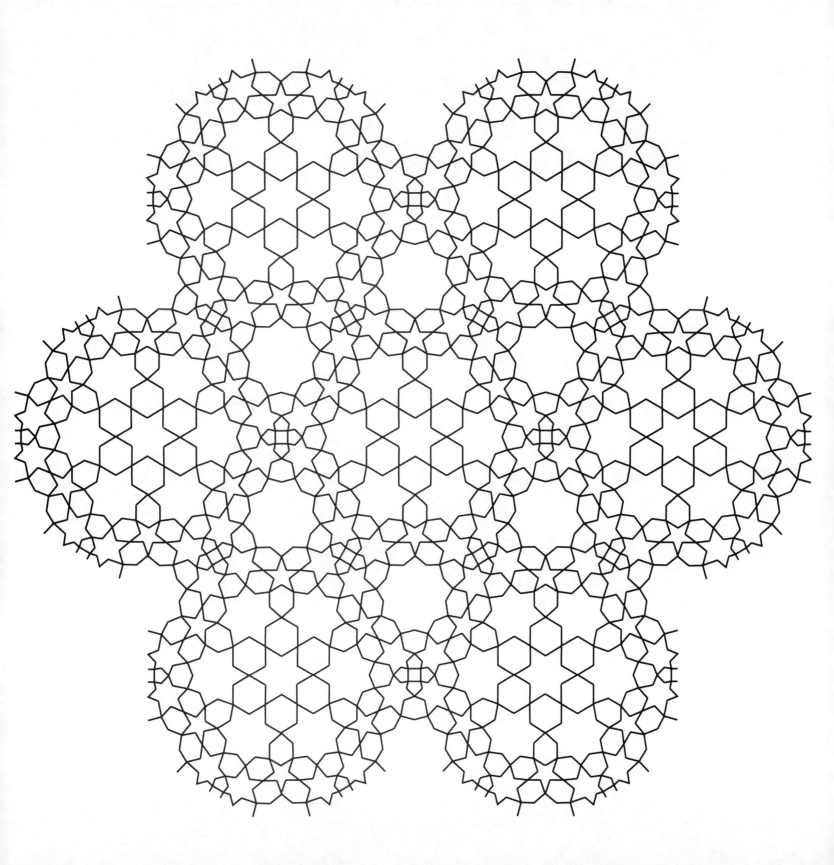

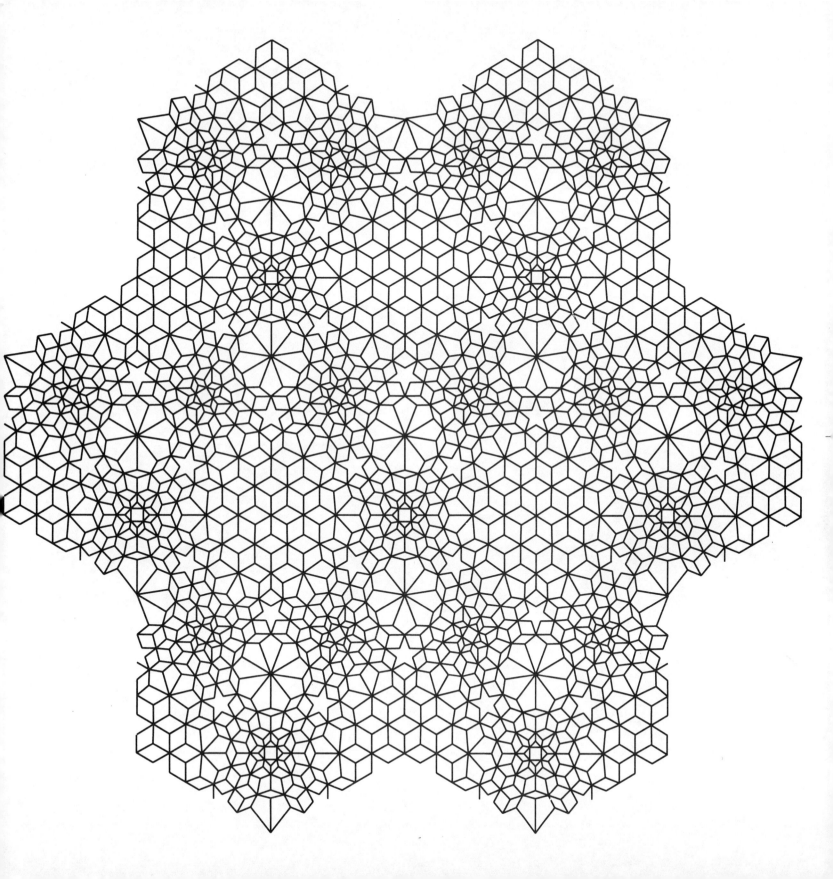

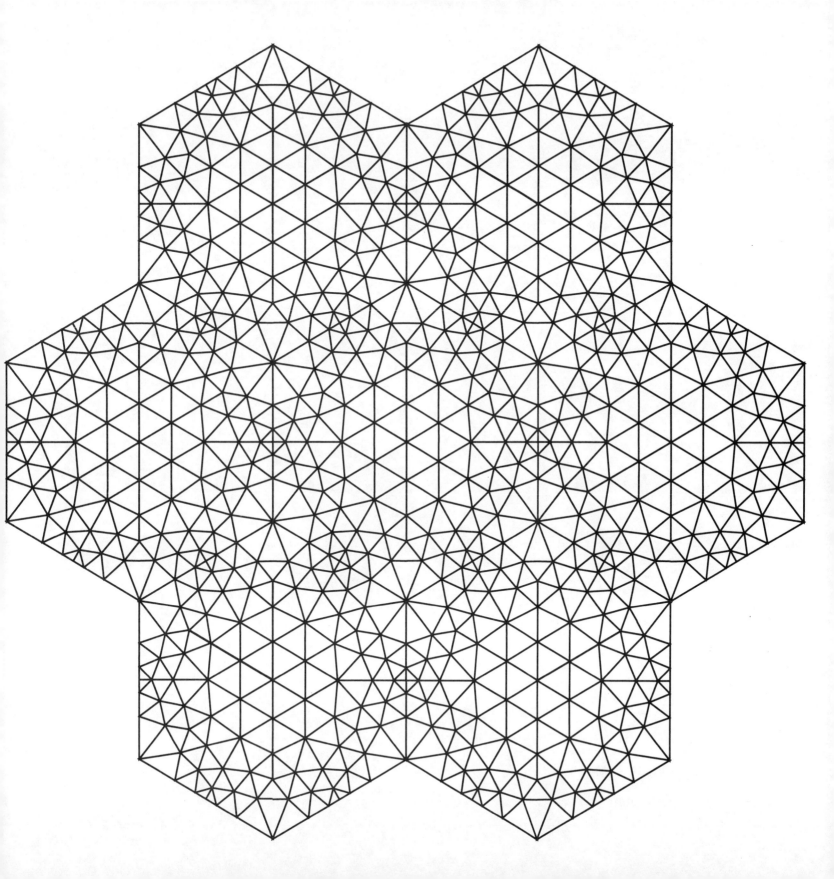

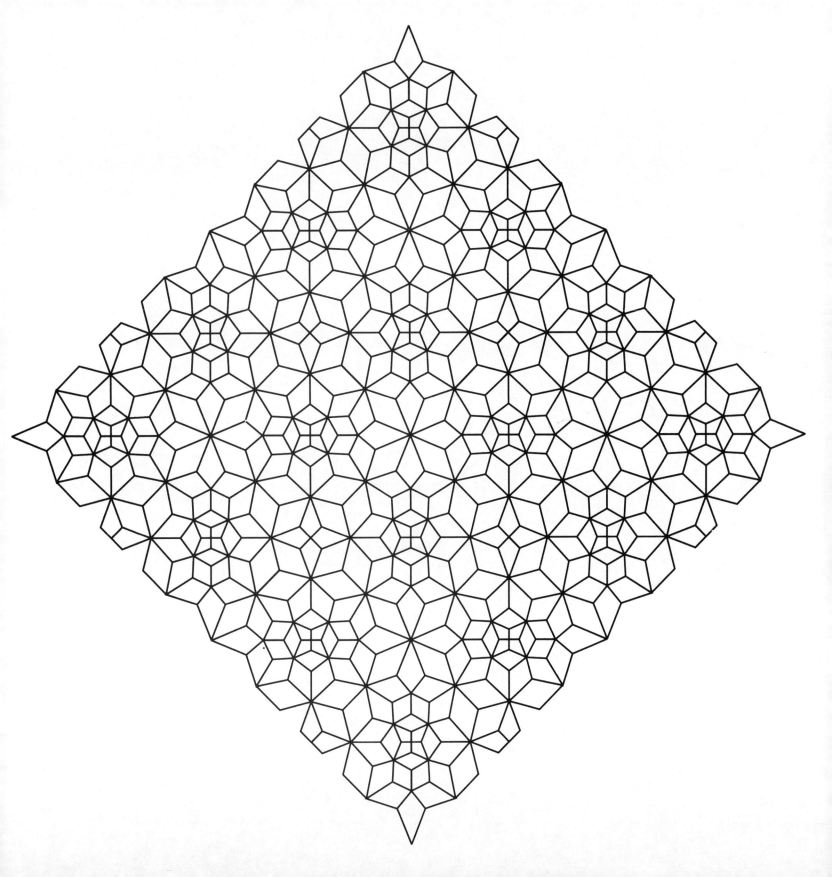

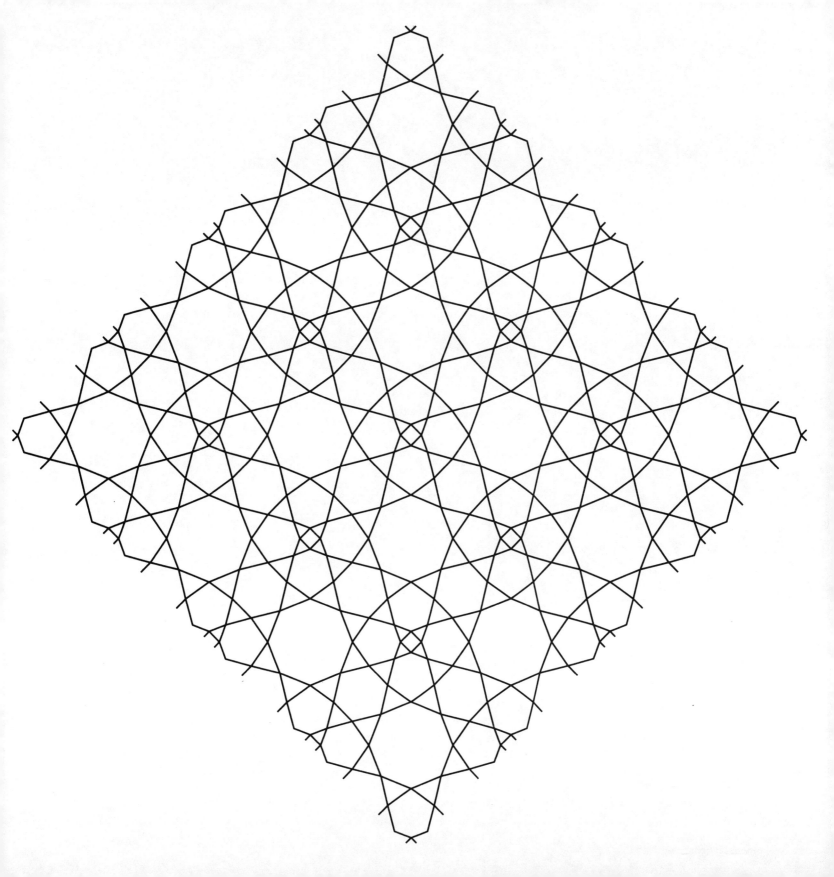

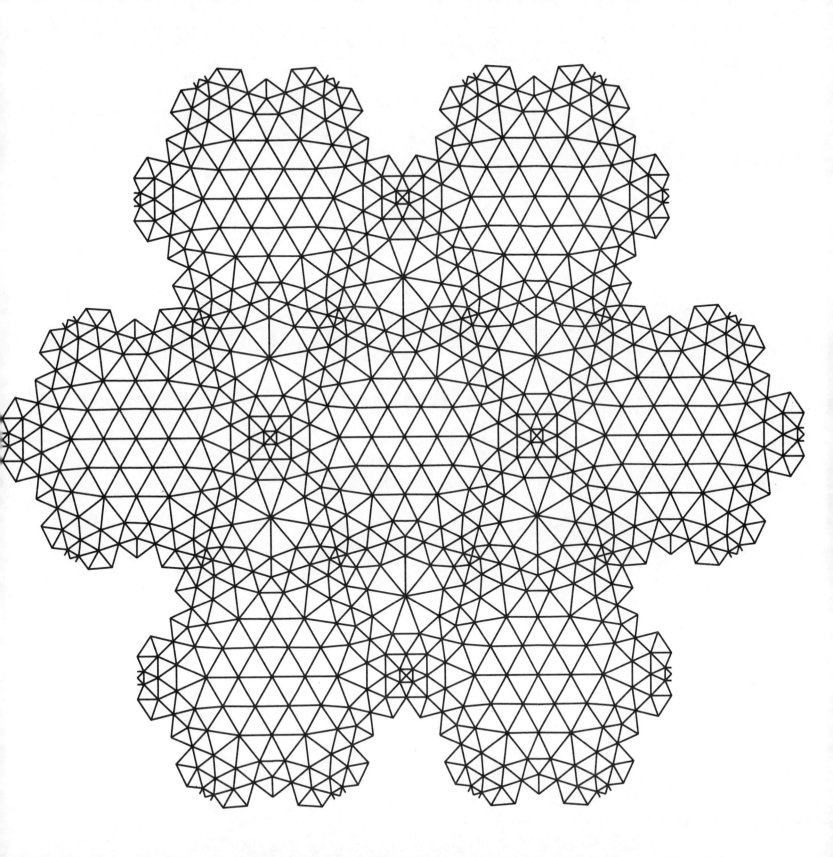

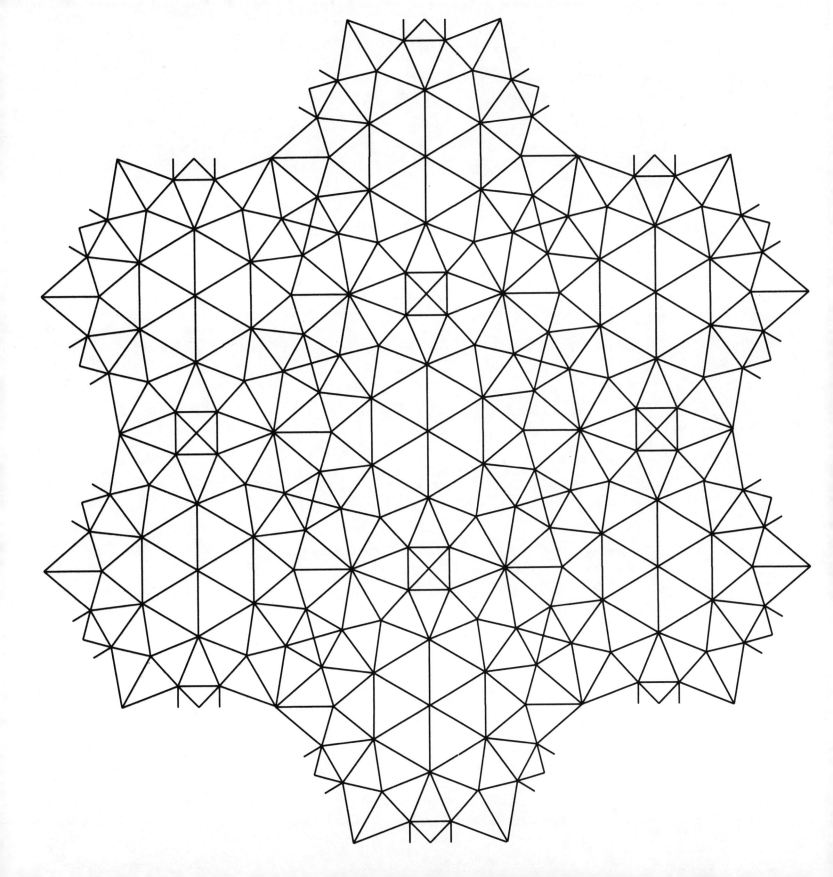

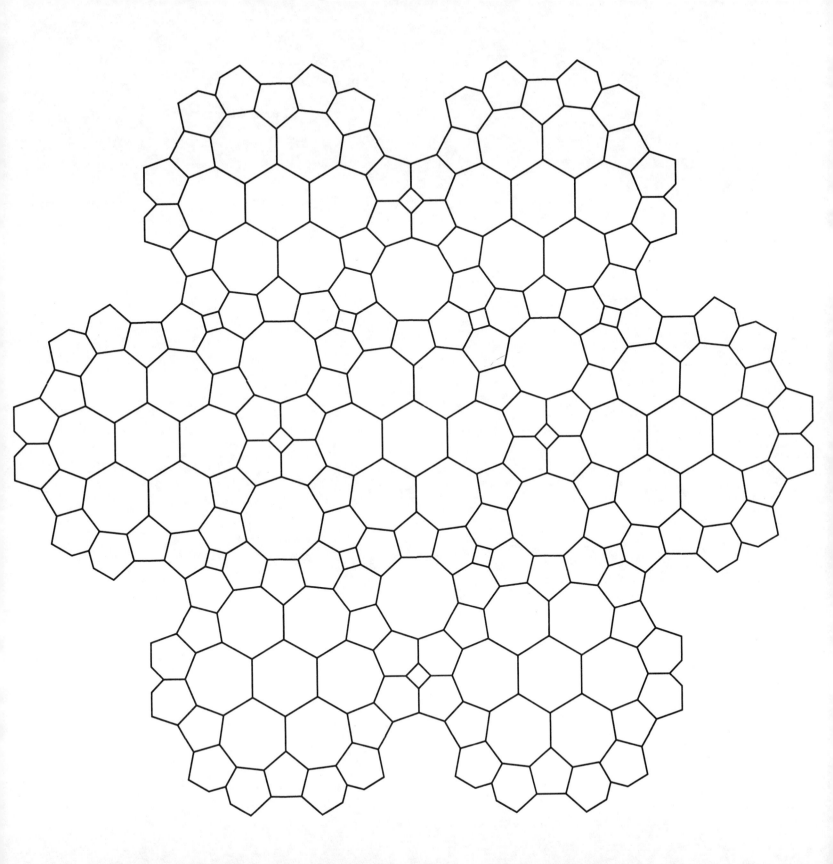

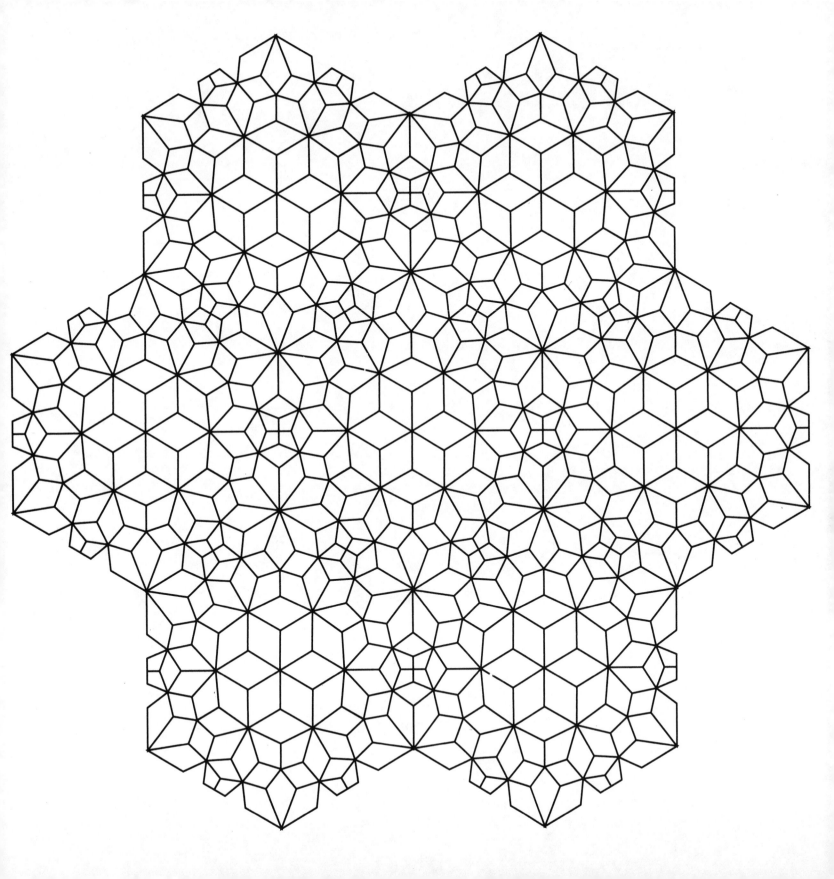

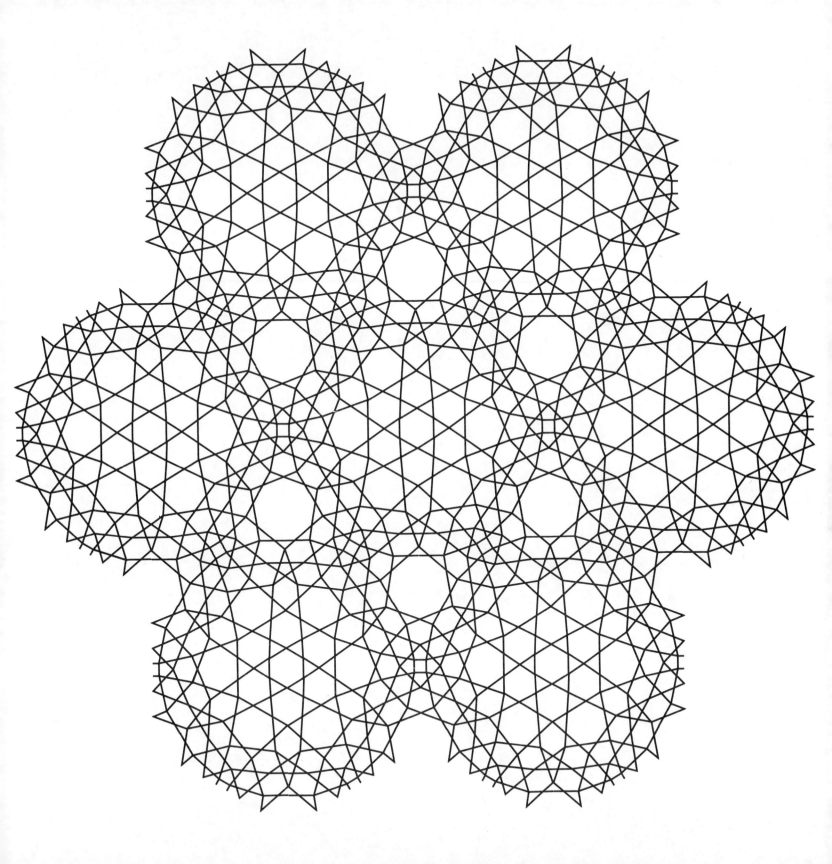

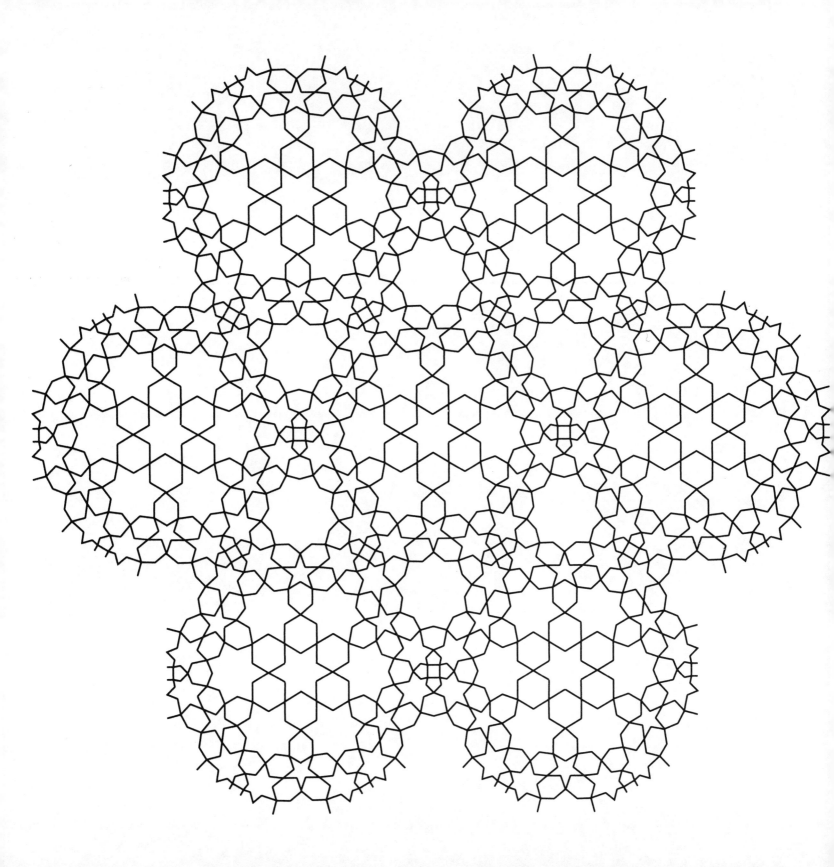

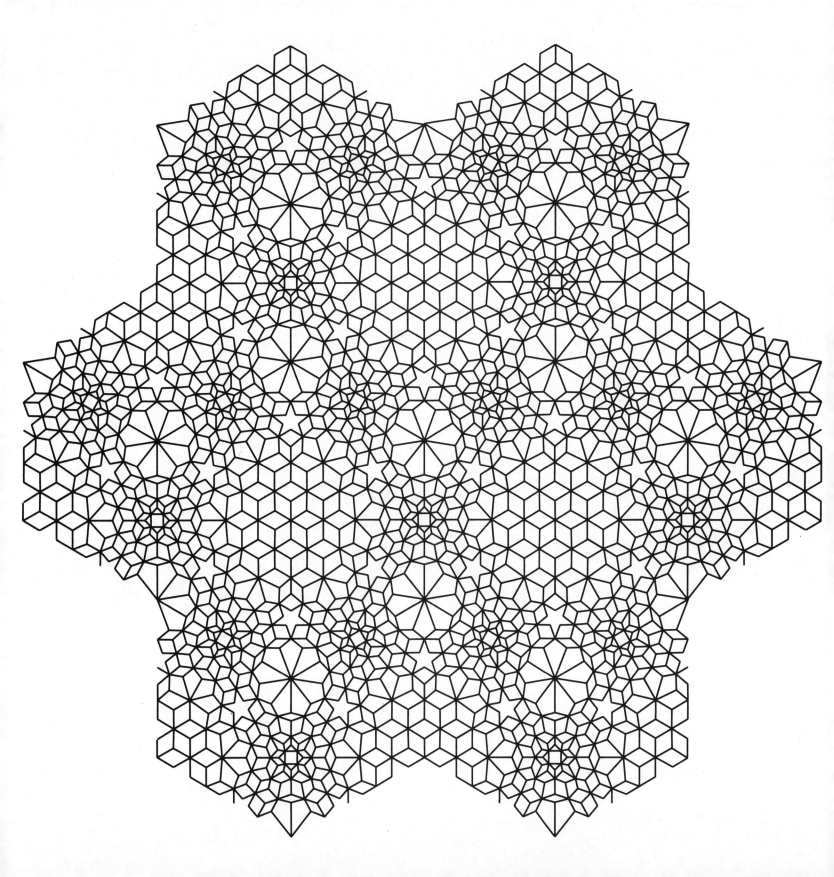

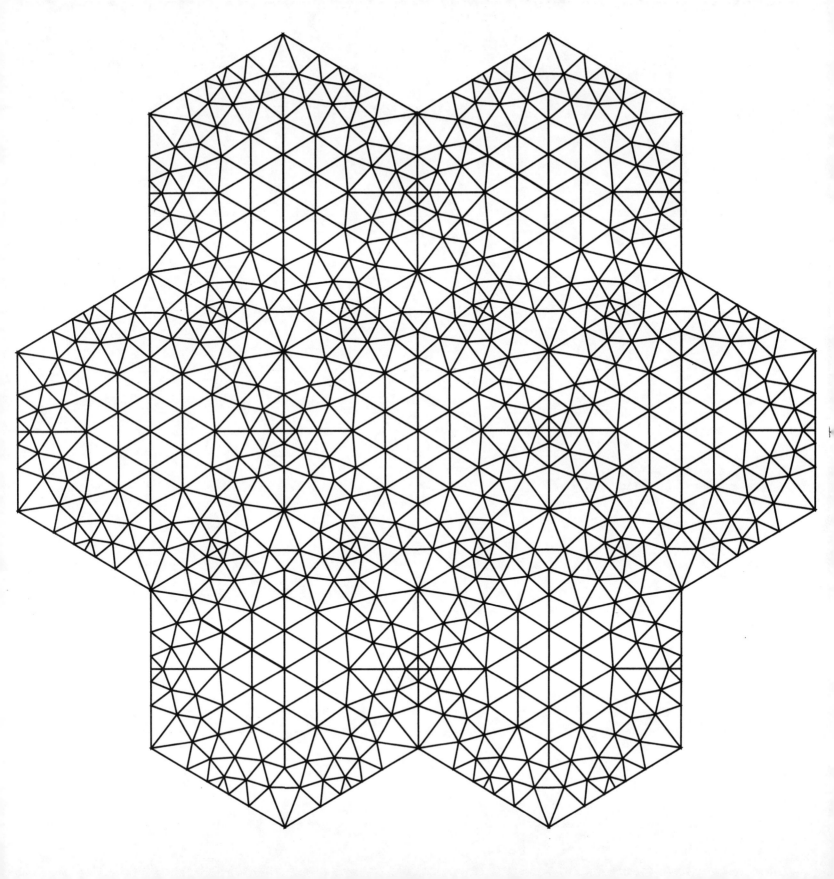

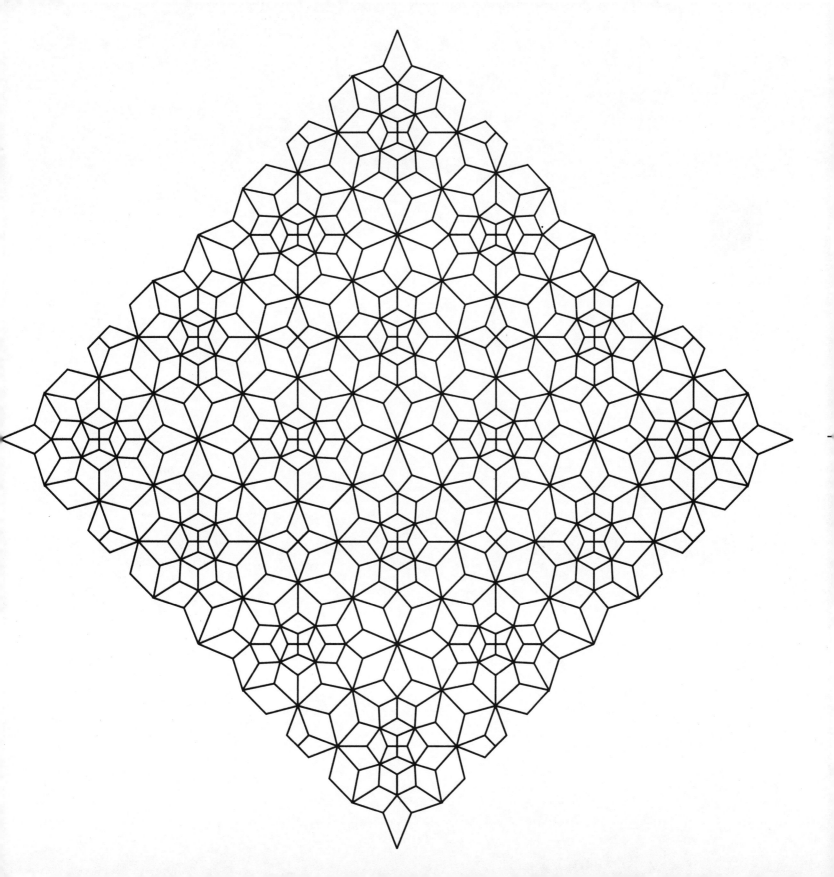

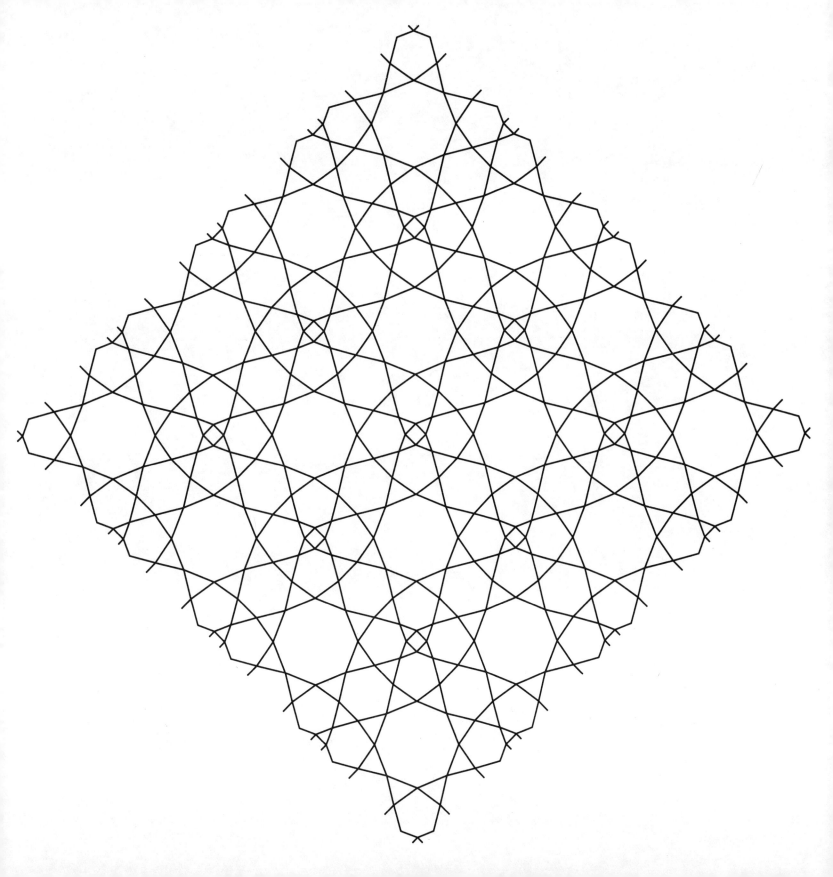